# INTEGRATING
## *Thinking*

### Practical Strategies & Activities To Encourage High-Level Responses

**Grades K through 12**

**BERTIE KINGORE**
AUTHOR

**Jeffery Kingore**
GRAPHIC DESIGN

**PROFESSIONAL ASSOCIATES PUBLISHING**

*Other Publications by*
# Bertie Kingore, Ph.D.

Alphabetters: Thinking Adventures with the Alphabet (Learning Task Cards)
Assessment: Time Saving Procedures for Busy Teachers, 2nd Ed.
Engaging Creative Thinking: Activities to Integrate Creative Problem Solving
Kingore Observation Inventory (KOI)
Literature Celebrations: Catalysts for High-Level Book Responses
Portfolios: Enriching and Assessing All Students; Identifying the Gifted, Grades K through 6
Reaching High Potentials
Teaching without Nonsense: Activities that Encourage High-Level Responses
We Care: A Preschool Curriculum for Children Ages 2 through 5

FOR INFORMATION OR ORDERS CONTACT:

**PROFESSIONAL ASSOCIATES PUBLISHING**
PO Box 28056
Austin, Texas 78755-8056
Phone/FAX: 512 / 345-6103

# INTEGRATING THINKING:
## *Practical Strategies and Activities to Encourage High-level Responses*

Grades K through 12

Second Printing, 1999

Copyright © 1999 Bertie Kingore

Published by **Professional Associates Publishing**

Printed in the United States of America
ISBN: 0-9657911-3-0

# TABLE OF CONTENTS

# INTRODUCTION ━━━━━━━━━━━━━━━━

*Integrating Thinking: Practical Strategies and Activities to Encourage High-Level Responses* is a book of learning experiences proven beneficial in hundreds of classrooms. As I developed, expanded, and modeled these with primary through secondary students, teachers commented on the simplicity and effectiveness of these activities. Educators would ask: "What book are these in?" and I would admit that I had not stopped to publish them. This book is a response to those teachers' enthusiasm for simple learning experiences that readily apply to multiple content areas and topics.

**PURPOSES OF THE STRATEGIES AND ACTIVITIES**

- To enable teachers to apply practical techniques and activities that stimulate students' thinking with less preparation time

- To provide a variety of simple strategies and activities that connect to a myriad of topics, content areas, and grade levels

- To serve as springboards for discussing and writing more extensively about a topic

- To celebrate diversity in thinking by encouraging students to respond with multiple correct ideas at different levels of understanding

- To relate the work being studied to students' lives and experiences

- To replace worksheet activities that require little thinking with tasks that encourage active participation and challenge students to generate new responses

- To assess students' depth and complexity of information

**GRAPHIC ORGANIZERS**

Many of the learning experiences in this book are graphic organizers that provide a visual representation of information. Use graphic organizers such as charts, graphs, and outlines to help students predict, explore, and expand concepts. Graphic organizers are used in many grade levels and content areas to illustrate students' depth of understanding and depict the relationship of the ideas or concepts. They are especially relevant for advanced or gifted learners who characteristically think in relationships, prefer to organize information in unique ways, and often have a depth of understanding beyond that of their age-mates (Kingore, 1995).

Kingore, B. (1999). Integrating Thinking. Austin, TX: Professional Associates.

Several graphic organizers are presented on the following pages. Venn variations, content puzzles, automaticity graphics, six boxes, and relation charts are adaptable to multiple content areas and topics. Teachers report that they are able to use each of these graphic organizers several times a year in different topics of study with only a minimum of preparation time.

These graphics prompt many educators to teach students to construct their own organizers. Advanced levels of learning are demonstrated when students produce original graphics to convey their ideas. The following list of attributes are provided to guide teachers and students in their development of effective graphic organizers.

### ATTRIBUTES OF EFFECTIVELY DEVELOPED GRAPHIC ORGANIZERS

- The format is clearly designed and easily understood by students.

- The form has the appropriate space needed for students' use.

- The organizer is designed to elicit high-level thinking.

- The form encourages students to integrate concepts and demonstrate skills.

- The form is open-ended to encourage diverse responses.

- Application of the graphic organizer generates discussion, elaboration, and expansion of ideas among students.

- The organizer is applicable to a myriad of content topics and grade levels.

### ASSESSMENT AND EVALUATION CONNECTIONS

1. Challenge students to use a graphic organizer to demonstrate the depth of their information about a topic rather than allowing them to simply lis facts.

2. Require a paragraph from each student elaborating and explaining the components on the graphic organizer.

3. Many of these learning experiences result in products to select for portfolios to document the student's mastery of a specified learning objective or topic.

4. As a variation that enhances analysis and discussion, provide a completed version of a graphic organizer with errors on it. In cooperative groups or as individuals, students locate and correct the errors.

Kingore, B. (1999). <u>Integrating Thinking</u>. Austin, TX: Professional Associates.

5. Develop rubrics that students and teachers use to evaluate the content and value of completed graphic organizers. Include levels of proficiency for each criterion. Share the completed rubric with students before they begin the learning task to clearly communicate expectations. In <u>Assessment: Time Saving Procedures for Busy Teachers</u> (Kingore, 1999), educators who need more concrete samples will find multiple assessment examples and a rubric generator to facilitate and simplify the process of creating rubrics. The attributes that follow are suggestions for graphic organizers' criteria.

## ATTRIBUTES OF EFFECTIVELY COMPLETED GRAPHIC ORGANIZERS

- Content relationships are evident.

- Ideas are clearly developed and organized.

- High-level thinking is apparent.

- Integrated skills are accurately applied.

- The response is diverse and exceeds typical or simple information.

- The response includes an appropriate degree of elaboration to clearly inform.

- In-depth content is incorporated.

- Complex ideas and concepts are evident.

## PROCESS AND PRODUCT MODELING

To enable maximum learning, the educator must teach students how to do each activity. Students can not be expected to work independently when they are uncertain how to complete the work successfully. They need modeling and successful experiences with a learning activity before they can proceed independently. The Modeling Learning Success chart on the next page outlines a sequence to guide students toward working independently. First, demonstrate the process with students participating as actively as appropriate. Then, facilitate the class through guided practice, and help students implement the process in pairs or small groups. These two initial steps are repeated until students can demonstrate they are ready to move toward more independence. The next level is individual application that requires students to work alone while the teacher facilitates. The final result of this sequence is that students can independently complete a process or product.

Discussion is an integral, continuous feature of this learning process. As students engage in discussion, their uncertainties can be clarified and their understanding enhanced both by the thoughtful questions posed by the teacher and by the interaction with other students.

Kingore, B. (1999). <u>Integrating Thinking</u>. Austin, TX: Professional Associates.

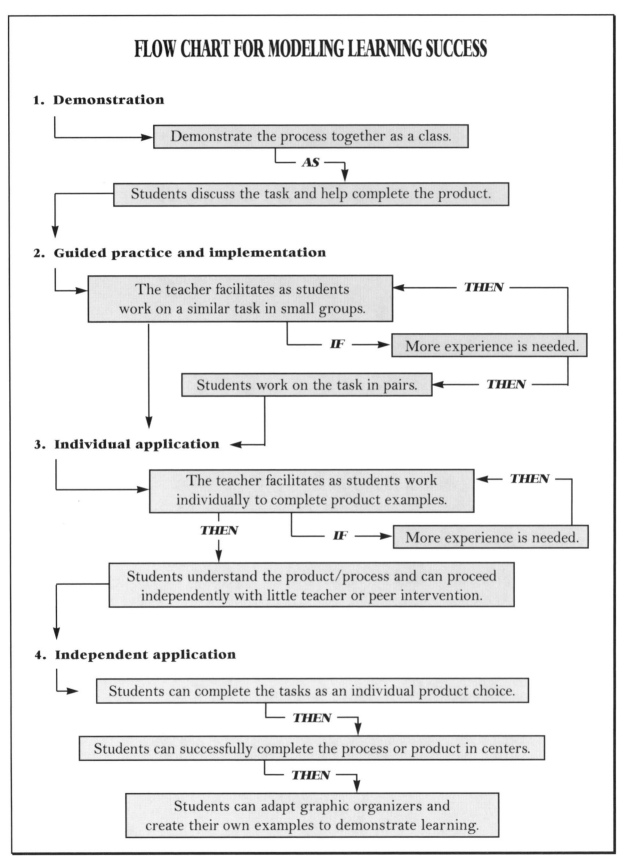

# FLOW CHART FOR MODELING LEARNING SUCCESS

**1. Demonstration**

Demonstrate the process together as a class.

*AS*

Students discuss the task and help complete the product.

**2. Guided practice and implementation**

The teacher facilitates as students work on a similar task in small groups.

*THEN*

*IF* → More experience is needed.

Students work on the task in pairs.

*THEN*

**3. Individual application**

The teacher facilitates as students work individually to complete product examples.

*THEN*

*IF* → More experience is needed.

Students understand the product/process and can proceed independently with little teacher or peer intervention.

**4. Independent application**

Students can complete the tasks as an individual product choice.

*THEN*

Students can successfully complete the process or product in centers.

*THEN*

Students can adapt graphic organizers and create their own examples to demonstrate learning.

Kingore, B. (1999). <u>Integrating Thinking</u>. Austin, TX: Professional Associates.

# INCREASING THINKING WITH BLOOM'S TAXONOMY

Every topic can encourage high-order responses when you use a list of thinking prompts incorporating Bloom's levels of thinking. These prompts allow teachers to insure success for all students by investigating the same topic in different ways at different levels of complexity.

Benjamin Bloom categorized thinking skills into six classifications evolving from the most basic, which is knowledge, to the most complex, evaluation. Lists of open-ended tasks and questions for literature, math, science, and social studies enable teachers to apply Bloom's Taxonomy to stimulate students' thinking with less preparation time. Teachers using these prompts report that in as little as five minutes they generate new ideas to integrate with their learning experiences for students. Completed examples applying this process to topics such as spiders, parts of speech, the "Three Little Pigs", and Miss Nelson Is Missing are included to model the possibilities.

## PURPOSE

1. To improve teachers' effectiveness in encouraging more complex responses from students

2. To involve students in developing high-order responses to instructional assignments

**GRADE LEVELS:** K-12

## DESCRIPTION

1. Select any book or topic you want to teach, and determine in which content areas you want to encourage higher-order thinking responses from your students.

2. Skim the Bloom's lists to help you brainstorm connections to that topic.

3. Use the prompts to directly incorporate topic words or as a checklist to help you brainstorm additional teaching connections. For example, sometimes the new idea you create is a result of completing one of the open-ended prompts with topic-related words. At other times, the prompts serve to help you think of a totally different idea. Review the provided examples for more specific guides to your own applications.

Kingore, B. (1999). Integrating Thinking. Austin, TX: Professional Associates.

**NOTES**

4. To reduce the number of pages, copy back-to-back the Bloom's applications for each curriculum area. Laminate each page, and keep it with your planning book. It will be convenient when new ideas are needed to uplift thinking.

5. Use your generated questions to lead discussions and your generated tasks to provide learning activities for your students. Be alert to additional questions and learning activities that are triggered by a student response or comment.

6. When appropriate, involve students in using the lists of thinking prompts to develop their high-order responses to instructional assignments. You can provide students with copies of the content area prompts shared here or develop shorter versions by selecting applicable items from each list for students to use.

7. Remember the strategy of providing a "wait time" of five or more seconds before expecting a response in order to allow students time for productive thinking. Teach students to use this strategy as they work together.

Using Bloom's Taxonomy is like constructing a stairway--each level serves as the foundation upon which the next higher level of thinking is built. More specifically, just as you could not build the fourth step of a stairway without the first three steps already being in place, students can not analyze something about which they have no knowledge, comprehension, or application. However, you do not have to start at the beginning levels of Bloom's on any learning experience for which children already have the background to respond at a higher level. The thinking prompts in this section are intended to enable instruction at each student's highest level of readiness.

In designating the level of Bloom's for each activity, the author identified the level most likely to be achieved by most students in most classrooms. Individual students may operate above or below the indicated level, depending upon the amount of thinking each applies to the task. The levels of synthesis and evaluation are obtainable only when teachers ensure that students incorporate analysis in their thinking process. Unless students analyze data and use that information to create a new idea or product, they are operating at the application level of Bloom's rather than at the higher level designated.

Kingore, B. (1999). Integrating Thinking. Austin, TX: Professional Associates.

# HIGHER-ORDER THINKING EXAMPLE FOR Miss Nelson Is Missing by James Marshall

**APPLICATION:**

1. Write a letter to Miss Nelson explaining why you miss her.
2. Construct a Missing Person report that lists the information concerning Miss Nelson's disappearance.
3. Draw a story board or comic strip portraying the sequence of events.
4. Present a newscast to report the happenings in Miss Nelson's class.

**ANALYSIS:**

1. Use a Venn Diagram to contrast the differences between how the children behaved for Miss Nelson and Miss Swamp.
2. Complete a story map for the book.
3. List three problems Miss Nelson had with her class. Then, illustrate and explain your ideas for solving each problem.
4. List all the clues that point to the fact that Miss Nelson truly is Viola Swamp.

**SYNTHESIS:**

1. Create a new story called "Miss Viola Swamp is Missing."
2. Write a want ad for the perfect substitute teacher.
3. Develop a recipe to change Miss Swamp into a great teacher. Use real ingredients to symbolize different features such as sugar for sweetness and Tabasco™ for spicy teaching ideas.
4. Create a persuasive speech to explain your idea of the ideal classroom.

**EVALUATION:**

1. Create an evaluation form and appraise Miss Nelson's disciplinary actions.
2. Debate the resolution: Miss Nelson's plan is the best way to make children behave.
3. Establish criteria for an ideal classroom. Rate your classroom and Miss Nelson's.
4. Read another book about Miss Nelson such as Miss Nelson Has a Field Day (1985). Establish criteria for evaluating whether the original story or the second book is better, and rate each.

# HIGHER-ORDER THINKING EXAMPLE FOR SPIDERS

**APPLICATION:**

1. Use yarn on a felt board to illustrate the process by which spiders spin a web.
2. Make a graph to show the sizes of spiders that live in the United States.
3. Survey 10 people to learn their opinion of spiders.
4. Make a chart to show the value and usefulness of spiders.

**ANALYSIS**

1. List five factors that influence people's opinion of spiders.
2. Use a Venn diagram to compare differences and similarities of two spiders.
3. Write and illustrate three analogies about spiders.
   A spider is like _____ because...
4. Determine how many different ways one might classify spiders.

**SYNTHESIS**

1. As rain forests are depleted, predict the outcome of the spiders that live there.
2. Write a worst case scenario for using insecticides to eradicate spiders.
3. Create and complete an observation process that does not disturb the natural habits of a spider common to your geographic area.
4. Specify the attributes that most fascinate you about spiders. Draw and label a new species of spider that incorporates each of those characteristics.

**EVALUATION**

1. Create a class presentation to share the results of your observation of a spider in its natural habitant and defend your conclusions from that observation.
2. Debate the use of insecticides.
3. Write a persuasive piece that justifies your opinion of spiders.
4. Explain the fallacies in the worst case scenarios others have hypothesized for using insecticides to eradicate spiders.

Kingore, B. (1999). Integrating Thinking. Austin, TX: Professional Associates.

## HIGHER-ORDER THINKING EXAMPLE FOR "The Three Little Pigs"

**KNOWLEDGE**
1. Name the main characters in the story.
2. Name two things that happened in the story.

**COMPREHENSION**
1. Describe the wolf as he stands outside the pigs' house.
2. Retell the story in your own words.

**APPLICATION**
1. Dramatize the scene when the first house is blown down.
2. Draw a map to show the route each pig travels.

**ANALYSIS**
1. Which parts of this story could be real and which are fantasy?
2. How is the wolf in the story different from the wolf in The True Story of The Three Little Pigs by Jon Scieszka?
3. In what way is the third little pig like his brick house?

**SYNTHESIS**
1. Rewrite and perform the story as a rap that ends with the theme or message of the story.
2. Suppose that the third pig lived in modern times and had a cell phone. Write a dialogue explaining who he calls and what happens.
3. Add yourself to the story and draw a picture to show your role.

**EVALUATION**
1. Which character in the story do you think displayed the highest moral standards in terms of our society? Explain and defend your choice.
2. Write an editorial defending either the wolf's or the third little pig's actions.

## HIGHER-ORDER THINKING EXAMPLE FOR PARTS OF SPEECH

**KNOWLEDGE**
1. List the eight parts of speech.
2. Repeat the definition of _____ (any part of speech).

**COMPREHENSION**
1. Show where the nouns (verbs; adjectives, etc.) are in this sentence.
2. Raise your hand each time you hear me read a conjunction (verb, etc.) in this paragraph.

**APPLICATION**
1. Write a sentence using all eight parts of speech.
2. Write an eight-word sentence using exactly five parts of speech.
3. Substitute new adjectives for each adjective in this poem.
4. Find a sentence on the sports page that contains an adjective and an adverb.

**ANALYSIS**
1. Diagram a sentence that uses all eight parts of speech.
2. Determine which part of speech is missing from this sentence/paragraph.
3. Which parts of speech are most often used in newspaper headlines? Which are least often used?

**SYNTHESIS**
1. Create a sentence with exactly ten words; diagram that sentence.
2. Write two sentences with different meanings that would be diagrammed the same.
3. Write an ambiguous sentence. Explain which part of speech makes it ambiguous.
4. "The dog chased the mailman." Rewrite that sentence to make it as long as you can while retaining meaning. Explain which parts of speech are most useful when elaborating.

**EVALUATION**
1. Debate the effectiveness of diagramming as a means to help people increase their writing ability.
2. Debate the usefulness of knowing and understanding the parts of speech.

Kingore, B. (1999). Integrating Thinking. Austin, TX: Professional Associates.

## LITERATURE: ▬▬▬▬▬▬▬▬▬▬▬▬▬▬▬▬▬
### INCREASING THINKING WITH ANY GOOD BOOK

**KNOWLEDGE**
1. Who is the main character?
2. Who is the author?
3. State two things that happened in the story.
4. List two other books by this author.
5. _____

**COMPREHENSION**
1. List two words used to describe the main character.
2. Describe the character's actions.
3. State one thing that happened in the beginning, the middle, and the end of the story.
4. Retell the story in your own words.
5. Find two other words that mean the same as _____.
6. Write a summary of the story.
7. _____

**APPLICATION**
1. Create a time line to show _____.
2. Write a letter to the main character.
3. Illustrate the turning point or climax of the story.
4. Demonstrate how the main character _____.
5. Act out one scene or event.
6. Draw an illustration relating the main events.
7. Select music to play in the background as you read one scene.
8. Create a poster that tells about the author.
9. _____

**ANALYSIS**
1. Name two characters (events; versions). How are they similar/different?
2. Could this really happen? What in the print makes it so?
3. Compare the main character with yourself.
4. Compare the setting to modern times; how would things be different?
5. How would you solve the problem in the story differently?
6. The main character or topic is like a(n) _____ because _____.
7. Identify which parts are real or fantasy; fact or opinion.
8. What is the main idea? What is the message implied by the story?
9. Select music that symbolizes the main character to play as you read one scene.
10. On a concept map, illustrate the characters' reactions and relationships.
11. What other books have similar messages/themes? Explain.
12. Use a Venn Diagram to compare this author's style to the style of your favorite author.

Kingore, B. (1999). <u>Integrating Thinking</u>. Austin, TX: Professional Associates.

13.  Compare this book to another one by the same author.
14.  Complete a story map relating the problem, main events in sequence, and the solution.
15.  _____
16.  _____

**SYNTHESIS**
1.  Predict what might happen if _____.
2.  Add yourself to the original story or historical times and write about your role.
3.  Create a new character or new event, and dramatize how it influences the original story.
4.  Create a new setting and time for the story which better suits the characters' needs.
5.  Create a museum exhibit that incorporates the most significant events in the book.
6.  Write a sequel to the book that shows how the character matures.
7.  Draw symbols for the main idea and events of the story.
8.  Make a collage using symbols for characters and events in the story.
9.  Write a diamante poem comparing the two main characters.
10.  Create a board game based on the most significant characters and events in the book.
11.  Draw a symbol for each character which reveals his/her most significant trait.
12.  Transform the text to perform as a choral reading or readers theater.
13.  Create a rap that relates the main events and ends with the theme of the book.
14.  Create an award for this book and explain the award's significance.
15.  _____

**EVALUATION**
1.  Write a review of this book for your local newspaper, evaluating the book's appropriateness and appeal for _____ aged readers.
2.  Judge the character according to your life standards.
3.  Did the main character make the right decision? Justify your answer.
4.  Would the outcome be plausible in a different time? Defend your view.
5.  After reading the story, assess the values that were modeled and determine what relationship those values have to your own life.
6.  Is the theme relevant for today's youth? Defend your position.
7.  Which character was most important to the story? Explain the criteria you used and defend your decision.
8.  You are an agent for the author. Convince a publisher to buy this book.
9.  Debate whether or not this book will be valued as a classic by future generations.
10.  This book is going to be made into a movie.
     a.  Create a new title and promotional poster for the movie that significantly promotes the message or theme.
     b.  Cast the movie, and defend how each of your casting choices matches each character.
     c.  Because of budget limitations, one character's role has to be eliminated. Defend which character can be deleted without significantly altering the story.
11.  _____
12.  _____

Kingore, B. (1999). Integrating Thinking. Austin, TX: Professional Associates.

## MATH: ▬▬▬▬▬▬▬▬▬▬▬▬▬▬▬▬▬▬▬▬▬
### USING BLOOM'S TAXONOMY TO INCREASE THINKING

### KNOWLEDGE
1. Read the _____.
2. Name the _____.
3. Count how many _____.
4. What is this sign?
5. Sing the _____ tables. (The tune for "Farmer in the Dell" is one possibility.)
6. Label the parts of the problem.
7. Repeat _____.
8. Tell some facts about _____.
9. _____
10. _____

### COMPREHENSION
1. Match the numeral and set.
2. Define and calculate _____.
3. In your own words, tell _____.
4. Show me the _____.
5. What is the value of _____.
6. Add the _____.
7. Demonstrate how many _____.
8. Explain greater than and less than in your own words.
9. _____
10. _____

### APPLICATION
1. Label your problem.
2. Arrange results according to _____.
3. Using what you have learned about this, how would you solve _____.
4. Sequence the fractions.
5. Put the data on a graph.
6. Find another set of objects that is equal.
7. Solve a problem in which ratio is used.
8. Classify by _____, and chart the data.
9. Using multiples, construct _____.
10. Give an example in a real life situation where a six by nine area is used.
11. Write another problem like this one.
12. Show me another way to total _____.
13. _____
14. _____
15. _____

Kingore, B. (1999). Integrating Thinking. Austin, TX: Professional Associates.

## ANALYSIS

1. What are variables?  What stays constant?
2. Determine the pattern.
3. How can you group these so they will _____.
4. Compare addition and multiplication.
5. Make a graph that contrasts _____.
6. Prepare a chart that categorizes _____ in two or more ways.
7. Demonstrate how the problem can be solved with fewer steps.
8. Explain how division relates to subtraction.
9. Add one to each number.  What do you notice?
10. What else would you need to know to solve this?
11. Which operation should be used to solve this problem? Explain why.
12. Identify two different sets of fractions that could be multiplied together to give an answer less than one. Explain how you determined those fractions.
13. _____
14. _____

## SYNTHESIS

1. Demonstrate how to get the same result following a different procedure.
2. Predict results if _____ was _____.
3. Forecast what would happen to stock markets if _____.
4. Reconstruct the problem so that it _____.
5. Create a new _____.
6. Design a test to determine if students understand the problem or math concept.
7. Develop a procedure to explain division to a younger student.
8. Create a presentation for the class about other mathematical concepts related to this.
9. Design a clear diagram identifying the most important elements of that process.
10. _____
11. _____
12. _____

## EVALUATION

1. Defend two ways your problem can be improved or completed differently.
2. Judge the best use of _____ in _____.
3. Pose criteria, and evaluate your own strengths and weaknesses in math.
4. Defend why you think this will work.
5. Critique _____ for clarity and interest.
6. Evaluate your prediction.
7. Defend your new way to solve the problem.
8. Create five problems, rate them according to difficulty, and defend your ratings.
9. On a scale of one to ten, judge how well you think you understand _____. Explain why.
10. _____
11. _____
12. _____

Kingore, B. (1999). Integrating Thinking. Austin, TX: Professional Associates.

## SCIENCE: ━━━━━━━━━━━━━━━
## USING BLOOM'S TAXONOMY TO INCREASE THINKING

**KNOWLEDGE**
1. What is the definition of _____?
2. What do you see?
3. List the objects _____.
4. Find the word that is _____.
5. List three characteristics.
6. List the steps _____.
7. Name the _____.
8. Label the parts of _____.
9. _____
10. _____
12. _____

**COMPREHENSION**
1. Write a paragraph explaining the concept we just read.
2. What caused this to happen?
3. Explain the meaning of _____.
4. Tell me in your own words _____.
5. Use these new science terms together in a sentence.
6. Which sense are you using to tell _____?
7. Explain why _____.
8. Name items that will _____.
9. What happened first in our experiment?
10. _____
11. _____
12. _____

**APPLICATION**
1. Discuss another time this has happened or might happen.
2. Make a chart to show _____.
3. Use this information to build a different _____.
4. What uses do we have for these objects?
5. Collect samples of _____.
6. Demonstrate the first step of the experiment.
7. Make a graph of _____.
8. Make a model of _____.
9. Illustrate the process.
10. _____
11. _____
12. _____

Kingore, B. (1999). Integrating Thinking. Austin, TX: Professional Associates.

**ANALYSIS**
1. List five factors which might influence _____.
2. Compare differences and similarities of _____.
3. What is the most important thing you learned from the experiment?
4. What made your experiment work?
5. Analyze each step of the experiment.
6. Analyze the pattern _____.
7. Prepare a chart that categorizes _____.
8. Illustrate the attributes it has but does not need to have to be classified as _____.
9. _____ is like _____ because _____.
10. Determine three different ways to classify these.
11. Prepare a flow chart that contrasts _____.
12. What else would you need to know to solve this?
13. _____
14. _____
15. _____

**SYNTHESIS**
1. Predict the outcome of _____.
2. Imagine the situation in 10 years.
3. Form a hypothesis _____.
4. Specify attribute changes and design a new _____.
5. Write a worst case scenario for _____.
6. Create a _____ using _____.
7. Create an observation process that does not disturb the natural habits of _____.
8. Develop a procedure to explain this principle to a younger student.
9. Create a presentation for the class about other related science concepts.
10. _____
11. _____
12. _____

**EVALUATION**
1. Support the reasoning behind your facts or hypothesis.
2. Develop two ways to test your hypothesis and determine which is better.
3. What in the experiment validated that you were correct?
4. What are the ethics involved in this discovery or procedure?
5. Validate the best solution.
6. Defend why consistent standards are important for the valid results of an experiment.
7. Defend your conclusions to a board of scientists.
8. Justify your opinion on _____.
9. Consider five scientific principles. Rate them according to difficulty.
10. _____
11. _____
12. _____

Kingore, B. (1999). Integrating Thinking. Austin, TX: Professional Associates.

## SOCIAL STUDIES: ▬▬▬▬▬▬▬▬▬▬▬
### USING BLOOM'S TAXONOMY TO INCREASE THINKING

**KNOWLEDGE**
1. Match the _____.
2. State the definition of _____.
3. Name the events that led to _____.
4. List the characteristics of _____.
5. Name the populations that _____.
6. List the geographic characteristics of _____.
7. Name two explorers discussed in this chapter.
8. _____

**COMPREHENSION**
1. Paraphrase the events.
2. State in your own words what _____ means.
3. Read the graph/table, and tell _____.
4. Discuss the reasons for _____.
5. Explain the conflict that _____.
6. Explain one resource of _____.
7. Discuss the plight of _____ during _____.
8. _____

**APPLICATION**
1. Make a time line to show _____.
2. Draw a map to show _____.
3. Make a graph to show _____.
4. Illustrate the steps _____ went through to _____.
5. Make a flow chart listing the communications events that led to _____.
6. Set up an opinion poll regarding _____.
7. Use the principles of economics in solving _____.
8. Apply historical facts of _____ to today's _____.
9. Apply pluralism to the political issue of _____.
10. Show how the _____ of the period gave us a picture of today's _____.
11. _____
12. _____
13. _____

**ANALYSIS**
1. Tell three similarities and differences of _____.
2. Analyze the relationships among _____.
3. Use a Venn diagram to compare _____.
4. Which natural resources were most valuable in enabling _____ to _____?

Kingore, B. (1999). Integrating Thinking. Austin, TX: Professional Associates.

5.  Analyze the social problems of _____.
6.  Analyze the public issue of _____.
7.  Connect the elements that led to _____.
8.  Compare the lifestyles of _____ and _____.
9.  What do the artifacts of _____ infer about their civilization?
10. Determine three causes leading to _____.
11. _____
12. _____

## SYNTHESIS

1.  Make a diorama of the life and customs of _____.
2.  Write an essay combining elements of _____ and _____.
3.  Write and perform a puppet show discussing the need for _____.
4.  Create a role playing scenario depicting the major cause of _____.
5.  Develop a compromise for _____.
6.  Establish a community advisory committee that _____.
7.  Develop a political system for _____.
8.  Plan an economic system for _____.
9.  Rewrite _____ from the point of view of _____.
10. Predict future issues for _____.
11. Propose a plan for, _____ and sequence its _____.
12. Compose a flow chart to relate what might occur if _____'s environment was changed to _____.
13. Propose an alternative to _____.
14. _____
15. _____

## EVALUATION

1.  Justify the conclusion that _____.
2.  Create new symbols for _____ and justify your choices.
3.  Evaluate the most significant moral development of that period.
4.  Judge the arguments for and against _____.
5.  Defend the social changes of _____.
6.  Evaluate the culture of _____.
7.  Evaluate the contributions of _____.
8.  Explain the fallacies of _____, and substantiate your stand.
9.  Defend the policy of _____.
10. Justify the aggression of _____.
11. Debate the resolution _____.
12. Conduct a trial in which the jury determines the fate of a historical figure for his or her actions.
13. _____
14. _____

Kingore, B. (1999). <u>Integrating Thinking</u>. Austin, TX: Professional Associates.

# CONTENT PUZZLES

## PURPOSE

1. To encourage students to apply reading, writing, thinking, and fine motor skills in multiple content areas

2. To serve as springboards for reviewing information and discussing a topic

3. To assess students' accuracy, depth, and complexity of information

**GRADE LEVELS:** 1-12

## DESCRIPTION

Content puzzles are a manipulative graphic organizer that combine thinking skills and fine motor skills. Key facts are written within a simple outline. The shape is then cut into puzzle pieces. As students reassemble the puzzle, they analyze syntactic relationships and review important content. Some completed examples and blank forms of content puzzles are included to model possibilities.

Begin modeling the process by having students work puzzles you have created. Then, teach students how to develop their own puzzles for exchanging with peers. Students are very motivated to include challenging and often complex content when they prepare a task for peers to work. Many students reread resources and spend more time considering content to include on their puzzles. When students work in small groups to develop original content puzzles, the activity encourages extensive discussion about the topic.

Designate the skills or content you want students to incorporate on a puzzle so the focus is on information rather than puzzle skills. As a specific example, the rectangle puzzle with math equations requires students to perform math computations and line up the problems on the correct rectangles. Students have to accurately solve the math problems to know if the rectangles are in their appropriate place. Students can not put the puzzle together correctly without concentrating on math.

Kingore, B. (1999). Integrating Thinking. Austin, TX: Professional Associates.

The following are suggestions for content puzzle applications.

> - **Sentences using basic reading words**
> - **A how-to sequence**
> - **Retelling key events in a story or historical incident**
> - **Summarizing a process or story**
> - **Depicting causes and effects**
> - **Describing the life or traits of a person or character**
> - **Math facts**
> - **Affixes and roots to combine to form words**
> - **Matching homophone pairs, e.g., pear/pair**

Consider these points when you want students to experience success creating their own content puzzles.

- Initially, use the blank content puzzle forms for students to fill in, exchange, and work.

- Puzzles using shapes of specific figures, such as the Lincoln profile, the rocket, and the house, are somewhat simpler for students to complete than those with more abstract connections such as the rectangle and jig saw puzzles.

- For ease in handling, provide envelopes or small zip-lock ™ bags for each student to use when storing cut-out puzzle pieces.

- Have students write their names or initials on each cut-out piece so if one piece gets mixed up it can be returned.

- After students experience success with the blank content puzzle forms, have them draw their own shapes to use as a puzzle. Encourage them to think of shapes that clearly relate to the topic or content.

- To prevent students from creating 200 piece puzzles, specify into how many pieces students may cut their original puzzles!

- Require that some content be included on each puzzle piece to avoid blank, meaningless pieces.

**VARIATIONS**

1. GRAPHEME-PHONEME RELATIONSHIPS. Accent grapheme-phoneme connections by having primary students glue pictures of items beginning with the same sound on a cutout of the letter that represents that sound. Students then cut the letter into puzzle pieces for others to work.

Kingore, B. (1999). Integrating Thinking. Austin, TX: Professional Associates.

2. FACT FAMILIES. A similar task involves using cutouts of numerals. Students write equations that result in that number all over the large numeral before it is cut into a puzzle.

3. CONTENT DEPTH AND CHALLENGE. Multiple copies of the Rectangle Content Puzzle can be placed side-by-side to create a more complex puzzle and extend content depth and challenge.

4. PERSONAL CONTENT PUZZLES. Invite students to complete personal content puzzles similar to the example for Jason on the next page. They write several sentences about themselves on a large initial of their first names. Place the puzzles in small, numbered envelopes. The envelopes are effectively stored standing up in a small shoe box. Students number a sheet of paper to correspond with the total number of students in the class. Then, as students have extra time, they work one of the numbered puzzles and write, by the matching number on their paper, the student's name and one thing they learned about that student from working the puzzle. Personal content puzzles are a fun way to combine reading, writing, and spatial skills with effective activities that help students know more about each other.

5. PUZZLES WITH BOGUS PIECES. Increase the use of content puzzles to effectively assess information accuracy and depth by including extra pieces with inaccurate information. A teacher can easily see if students have selected only the pieces with valid data and left out the bogus pieces.

**Inaccurate pieces**         **Correct puzzle**

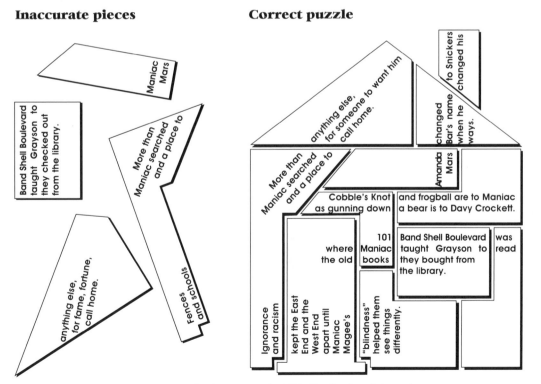

Kingore, B. (1999). <u>Integrating Thinking</u>. Austin, TX: Professional Associates.

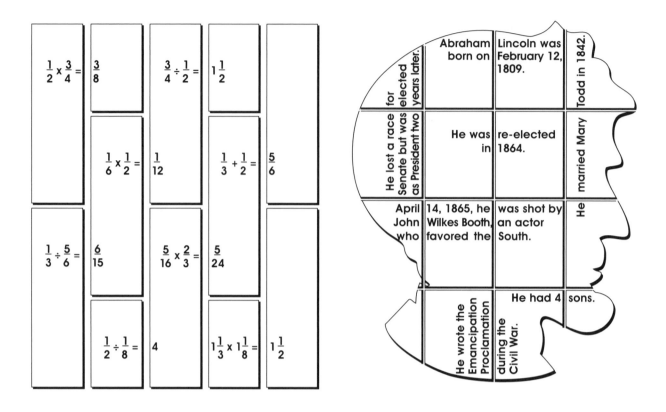

$$\frac{1}{2} \times \frac{3}{4} = \frac{3}{8}$$

$$\frac{3}{4} \div \frac{1}{2} = 1\frac{1}{2}$$

$$\frac{1}{6} \times \frac{1}{2} = \frac{1}{12}$$

$$\frac{1}{3} + \frac{1}{2} = \frac{5}{6}$$

$$\frac{1}{3} \div \frac{5}{6} = \frac{6}{15}$$

$$\frac{5}{16} \times \frac{2}{3} = \frac{5}{24}$$

$$\frac{1}{2} \div \frac{1}{8} = 4$$

$$1\frac{1}{3} \times 1\frac{1}{8} = 1\frac{1}{2}$$

Abraham Lincoln was born on February 12, 1809.

He lost a race for Senate but was elected as President two years later.

He was re-elected in 1864.

He married Mary Todd in 1842.

April 14, 1865, he was shot by John Wilkes Booth, an actor who favored the South.

He

He wrote the Emancipation Proclamation during the Civil War.

He had 4 sons.

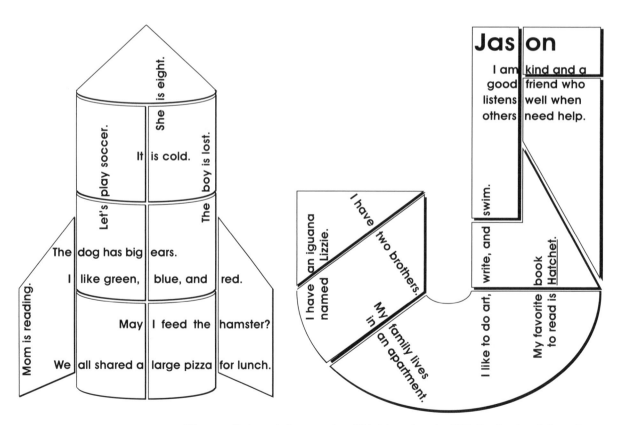

She is eight.

It is cold.

The boy is lost.

Let's play soccer.

The dog has big ears.

I like green, blue, and red.

May I feed the hamster?

We all shared a large pizza for lunch.

Mom is reading.

I have an iguana named Lizzie.

I have two brothers.

My family lives in an apartment.

**Jas on**

I am kind and a good friend who listens well when others need help.

I like to do art, write, and swim.

My favorite book to read is Hatchet.

Kingore, B. (1999). Integrating Thinking. Austin, TX: Professional Associates.

# CONTENT PUZZLE: ROCKET ━━━━━━━

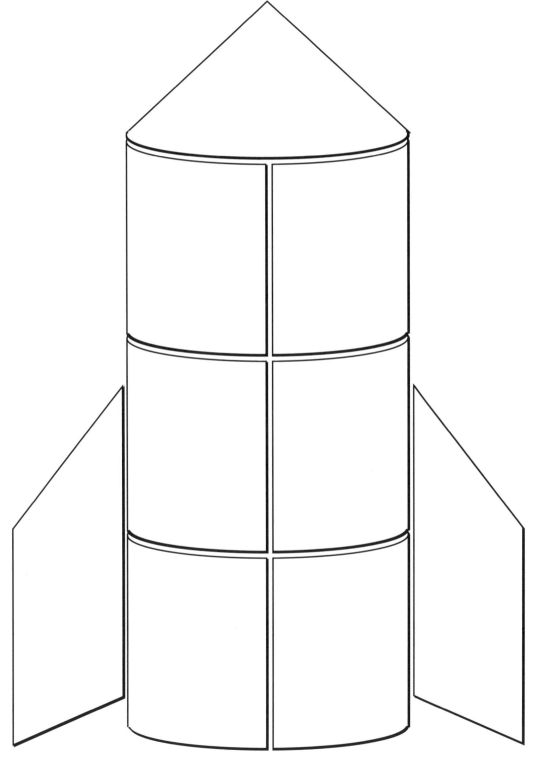

Kingore, B. (1999). <u>Integrating Thinking</u>. Austin, TX: Professional Associates.

## CONTENT PUZZLE: LINCOLN

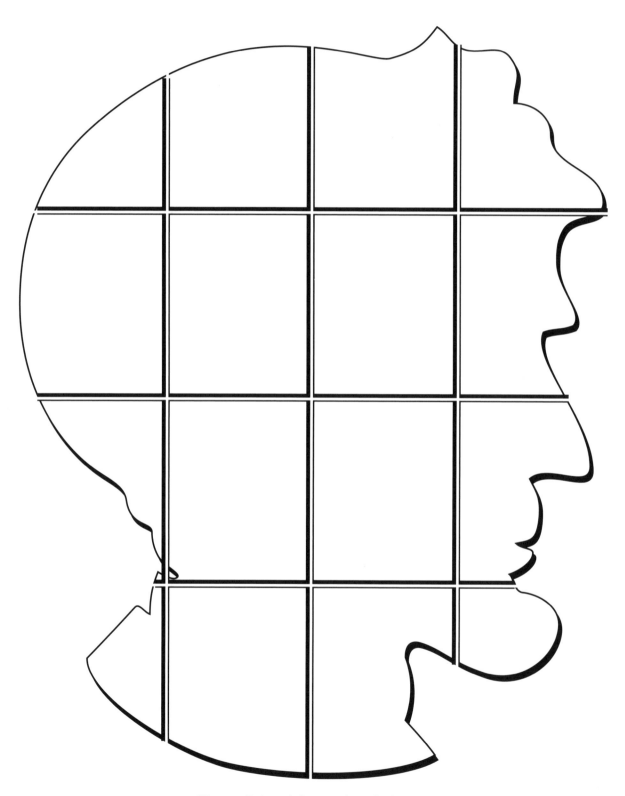

Kingore, B. (1999). Integrating Thinking. Austin, TX: Professional Associates.

# CONTENT PUZZLE: HOUSE

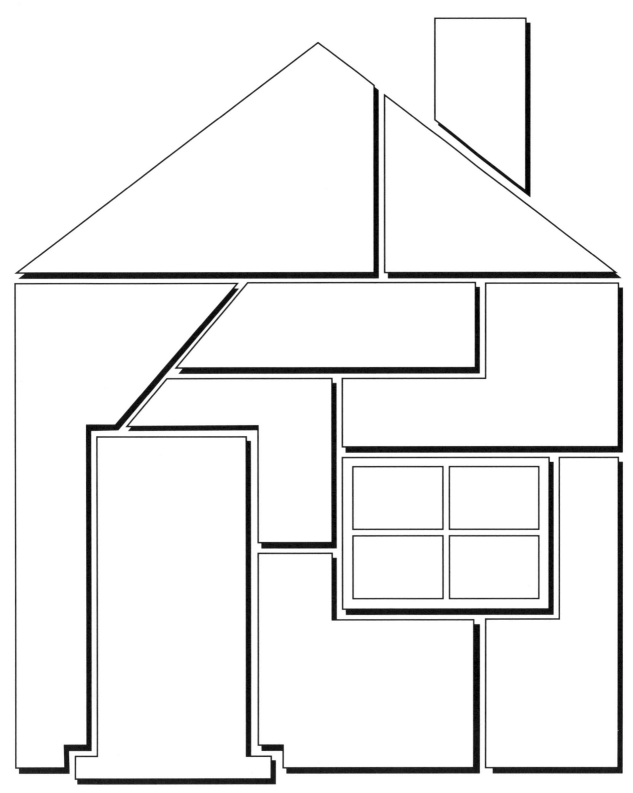

Kingore, B. (1999). <u>Integrating Thinking</u>. Austin, TX: Professional Associates.

# CONTENT PUZZLE: RECTANGLES

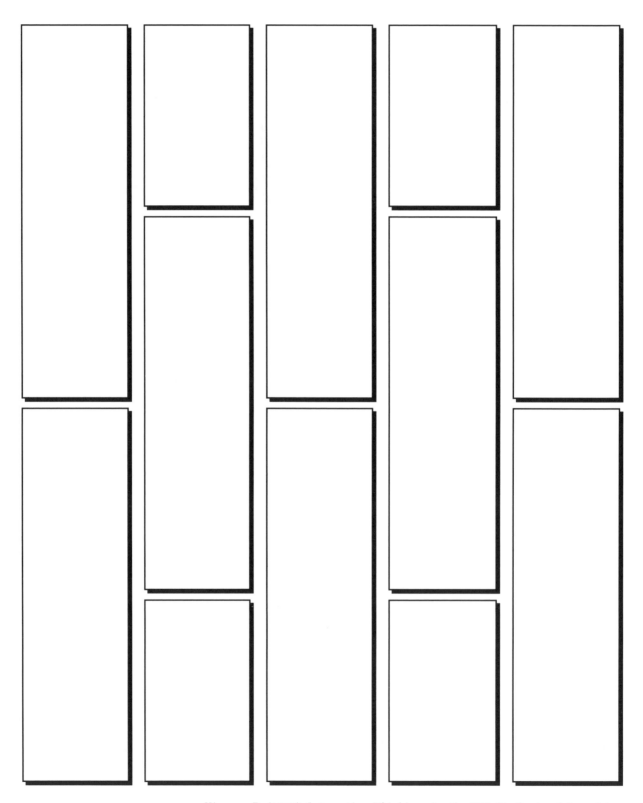

# CONTENT PUZZLE: JIG SAW

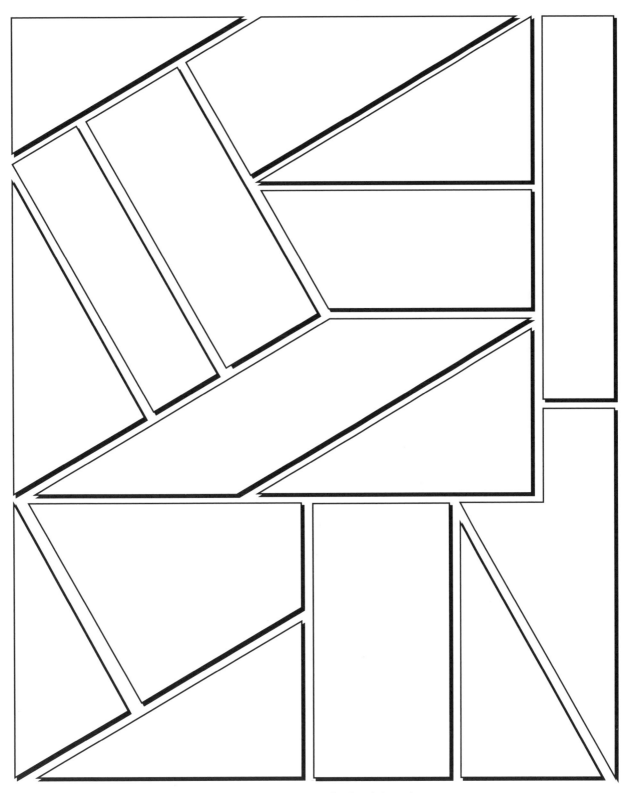

Kingore, B. (1999). <u>Integrating Thinking</u>. Austin, TX: Professional Associates.

# RELATION CHARTS ▬▬▬▬▬▬▬▬▬▬▬▬▬▬▬▬▬▬▬▬

NOTES

## PURPOSE

1. To encourage students' high-level thinking

2. To serve as springboards for discussing or writing more extensively about topics

## GRADE LEVELS: 3-12

## DESCRIPTION

Relation charts use guide words to explore relationships among the major elements of an issue, topic, story, or event. The charts are adapted from Schmidt's and Buckley's concept of Plot Relationship Charts for story structures (Macon, et al., 1991). Forms for three versions of relation charts and examples using each form are provided. Students' responses on the forms can be simple or more elaborate. The forms help students organize information to expand into summaries or longer expository responses. As a variation, write the guide words across the top of the chalkboard. Then, work together as a class to develop lists of multiple responses to each prompt for the story, event, or topic under study.

### RELATION CHART: PLOT ▬▬▬▬▬▬▬

NAME _Richard_                    DATE _January 8_
BOOK _Amazing Grace by Mary Hoffman_

| SOMEONE | Grace |
|---------|-------|
| **wanted** |
| to play the part of Peter Pan |
| **because** |
| she loves to act out adventures and fairy tales. |
| **However,** |
| her classmates tell her she can't be Peter Pan because Peter Pan isn't a girl and he isn't black. |
| **So,** |
| Grace's family helps her believe she can be anything she wants if she puts her mind to it, and Grace becomes an amazing Peter Pan. |

Kingore, B. (1999). Integrating Thinking. Austin, TX: Professional Associates.

## RELATION CHART: ISSUE

NAME _Elizabeth_   DATE _May 3_

ISSUE _Slavery in the United States of America_

| ONE VIEWPOINT IS | the Confederacy. |
| --- | --- |

**This view believed**

that some people were less than deserving of full-fledged human rights. Plantations maintained by slaves were part of the Confederate culture, and Southerners believed slaves were vital to the economic survival of the farming South.

| A SECOND VIEWPOINT IS | the Union. |
| --- | --- |

**This view believed**

that slavery was barbaric and demeaning. The Union believed the Declaration of Independence considers all races to be created equal and endowed by their Creator with certain unalienable rights.

**So,**

slavery became an antagonist of the Civil War, and the Confederacy seceded from the United States of America. After four years, the Confederacy surrendered and the war ended.

**Then,**

Abraham Lincoln's Emancipation Proclamation gave all races freedom, but in order to be reunited by the US government, each state had to ratify the Bill of Rights. The Eighth Amendment abolished all forms of slavery.

**Finally,**

over one hundred years later, our society is beginning to believe in the equality of people regardless of race and promote global under-standing instead of suspicion.

## RELATION CHART: TIME

NAME _Lynn_   DATE _April 26_

TOPIC _Transportation_

**PAST**

**In the past,**

people walked, rode animals, and used carts to carry what they needed.

**However,**

that was slow and sometimes harmed animals. People also had problems with heavy loads.

**PRESENT**

**So now,**

we have many kinds of vehicles that have engines or motors.

**The reason for this is**

they can move people and heavy loads rapidly.

**FUTURE**

**What will probably happen next is**

we will continue to research alternative sources of energy and develop very different transportation methods that are safe and extremely fast.

Kingore, B. (1999). <u>Integrating Thinking</u>. Austin, TX: Professional Associates.

# RELATION CHART: PLOT ━━━━━━

NAME _____     DATE _____

BOOK _____

| Someone |
| :--- |
| **wanted** |
| |
| **because** |
| |
| **However,** |
| |
| **So,** |

# RELATION CHART: ISSUE

NAME _____     DATE _____

ISSUE _____

| **ONE VIEWPOINT IS** |
|---|
| This view believes |

| **A SECOND VIEWPOINT IS** |
|---|
| This view believes |

| So, |
|---|

| Then, |
|---|

| Finally, |
|---|

Kingore, B. (1999). Integrating Thinking. Austin, TX: Professional Associates.

# RELATION CHART: TIME

NAME _____     DATE _____

TOPIC _____

| PAST | **In the past,** |
| --- | --- |
| | **However,** |

| PRESENT | **So now,** |
| --- | --- |
| | **The reason for this is** |

| FUTURE | **What will probably happen next is** |
| --- | --- |

# SIX BOXES

**PURPOSE**

To replace worksheet activities that require little thinking with active participation tasks that challenge students to generate responses

**GRADE LEVELS:** 1–8

**DESCRIPTION**

Use the six-box graphic or have students fold a paper into six boxes. Then, the teacher specifies the skills or learning tasks for students to incorporate in the boxes. Because students generate their own examples, a wider variety of responses at different levels of understanding and complexity result than when teachers produce the problems or examples for students to answer.

The six-box graphic or folded paper is very applicable to learning skills and tasks. Some suggestions follow to prompt your creative applications.

- List key facts or the most important things to remember.
- Write a sequence or how-to procedure.
- Summary: The first two boxes relate the beginning, the second two the middle, and the last two the end of the story or event.
- Record main events or issues.
- Interest survey: Students write or illustrate what they want to read, talk about, or learn about a topic.
- Organize math problems for students experiencing difficulty with fine motor control by having students write one problem in each box.
- Story board or illustrate scenes from a story.
- Math story problems: Students draw sets in each of the boxes on the left. They then trade papers and write a story problem to illustrate each set on their partner's paper.
- Compare and contrast items on the left side with items on the right.
- Compare synonyms and antonyms.
- Write math facts, e.g., equations that total eight.
- Draw different coins to total $1.00.
- Compare concepts such as sink and float.
- Illustrate greater than and less than.

Kingore, B. (1999). <u>Integrating Thinking</u>. Austin, TX: Professional Associates.

# SIX BOXES FORM

NAME _____ DATE _____

TOPIC _____

# AUTOMATICITY GRAPHICS

**PURPOSE**

To provide a vehicle that helps students fine-tune skills to the level of automaticity

**GRADE LEVELS:** K-6

**DESCRIPTION**

Automaticity means that students are able to use skills without having to stop and think about them. Sight words, memorized math facts, and tying ones shoelaces are examples of tasks often performed at the automaticity level. Teachers or students write the items for review on an automaticity graphic. Students then try to correctly identify each item and erase it so they "wash" the graphic clean. The graphic is easily "washed" when used as an overhead transparency or made into a laminated poster. After modeling how to use the graphics, continue the task in small groups or pairs so students are more actively involved. Prepare several laminate copies of an automaticity graphic. Students work in pairs to write the designated content on the graphic and then take turns identifying and wiping off the content data. Students love to wash the graphic and are eager to repeatedly practice skills in this format. Examples of skills that are applicable to automaticity graphics include phonics, numeral recognition, math facts, sight words, and affixes or roots.

Kingore, B. (1999). <u>Integrating Thinking</u>. Austin, TX: Professional Associates.

CAR
WASH

IDEA
DRIVE

© 1999 Jeffery Kingore

Kingore, B. (1999). Integrating Thinking. Austin, TX: Professional Associates.

**BUNNY
BATH**

Kingore, B. (1999). <u>Integrating Thinking</u>. Austin, TX: Professional Associates.

# LAUNDRY

© 1999 Jeffery Kingore

Kingore, B. (1999). <u>Integrating Thinking</u>. Austin, TX: Professional Associates.

# FAST THOUGHTS

**PURPOSE**

1. To encourage students' high-level thinking

2. To revitalize and mentally engage students with fast-paced interaction

3. To serve as springboards for discussions among students

**GRADE LEVELS:** 2-12

**DESCRIPTION**

Fast Thoughts is a strategy for transition times or to incorporate during a lesson when a quick change of pace is needed. A category is presented and students have a few seconds in which to brainstorm and list examples that begin with the designated alphabet letter and fit that category.

1. Make an overhead transparency of the Fast Thoughts. Put the transparency on the overhead with a paper covering it so only the title shows. Have students get a scrap of paper and tell them how many seconds they will have to respond as you move the paper down to show them each catagory.

2. Stress to your students that responses must fit the category and only use words that begin with the letter listed beside the task. Some students forget to match the letter unless reminded of that requirement.

3. Use a timer, and set the allotted time so it is fast enough to be energizing but long enough to be realistic for handwriting and thinking speeds. Either a fifteen, twenty, or thirty second time limit works well for most grade levels.

4. When time is up, discuss students' responses. Fast Thought tasks are intended to be open-ended so multiple answers are possible. Some examples of student responses are listed for each prompt.

5. Typically, use just one prompt in a setting. Later, when a break is needed, put the Fast Thoughts transparency on the overhead again. Students look forward to these tasks and know to get ready quickly as they will have little time to respond. They so enjoy the quick-paced challenges that they

Kingore, B. (1999). Integrating Thinking. Austin, TX: Professional Associates.

remember the last one completed and can always tell you which one the class is ready to do next.

Fast Thoughts can be completed orally, but it insures more active participation from more students when they are required to write a response before sharing. Assure students that content and ideas are the focus during Fast Thoughts rather than perfect handwriting and spelling. Explain to students that the number listed on each Fast Thought is a challenge number. They are encouraged to try to match or exceed that number in the designated time allotted. However, they are successful during Fast Thoughts if they concentrate and write at least one appropriate response.

Several higher-level thinking skills are consistently applied by students as they respond to Fast Thoughts prompts.

- **Fluency**--listing more than one item for a category

- **Categorization**--thinking of items that fit the designated category

- **Application**--relating categories to personal schema

Many content area topics can be applied with this strategy. Three examples are shared to model possibilities. "Pets" is a simple example using a topic-related word to organize responses. "Research" is a second example applying vocabulary and factors related to students learning to conduct independent studies. "Thinking Skills" is the most generic example organized using the letters of the alphabet. A follow-up task is included for each letter to explore the designated thinking skill.

After many experiences, some students are able to work in small groups and create their own Fast Thoughts for a topic being studied. Extensive discussion of the topic ensues as students develop tasks for classmates' responses.

## FAST THOUGHTS: PETS

**P**  **2 kinds of pets**
- puppy, pony, poodle, python

**E**  **1 thing pets do to survive**
- eat, exercise, explore

**T**  **3 words to describe pets**
- tiny, tidy, troublesome, tender-hearted, tiring

**S**  **2 places to find pets**
- shelters for animals, stores, seashore, shell

Kingore, B. (1999). <u>Integrating Thinking</u>. Austin, TX: Professional Associates.

## FAST THOUGHTS: RESEARCH

**R**    **3 words to describe research**
- rewarding, rigorous, rational, realistic, reasonable

**E**    **2 sources of information**
- experts, encyclopedia, e-mail

**S**    **2 kinds of information you can observe**
- solar, size, shape, stain

**E**    **2 research topics appropriate to your grade level**
- energy, electrical storms, extinct species

**A**    **1 example of a kind of data you can infer**
- attitudes, aptitude, attributes

**R**    **2 important steps in research**
- reading, reviewing, reporting findings

**C**    **3 ways to share what you have learned in your research**
- chart, compare or contrast, chat, correspondence

**H**    **1 important term used in research**
- hypothesis, holistic

## FAST THOUGHTS: THINKING SKILLS

**A**    **3 things that have teeth**
- alligator, ape, adults, animals, aunts

    ***Thinking skill:*** Prediction
Which item on your list do you think many people listed? Which item is least likely to have been thought of by others?

**B**    **2 things that break easily**
- bubbles, beads, budgets

    ***Thinking skill:*** Flexibility
Combine your list with others around you. Now, determine another category into which each item fits.

**C**    **4 things found at the zoo**
- camel, caramel popcorn, cats, cockatoo, coins

    ***Thinking skill:*** Criterion establishment
Rank your list. What criteria did you use?

**D**    **2 things that have legs**
- dog, deer, debutante, duck, David

    ***Thinking skill:*** Direct analogy
Circle one item on your list. Complete the analogy: "Teaching is like _____ because _____."

Kingore, B. (1999). Integrating Thinking. Austin, TX: Professional Associates.

**NOTES**

**E**  **2 things larger than a book**
- elevator, elephant, eagle, energy

    ***Thinking skill:*** Compare
    Circle one item on your list. Name three ways it is similar to a book.

**F**  **4 things you can eat**
- fruit, fish, fresh eggs, frogs, fried worms, frosties

    ***Thinking skill:*** Awareness of audience
    Which item on your list is least appropriate for a baby? Which is least appropriate for an 80 year old?

**G**  **2 things you can not see**
- goodness, God, graciousness

    ***Thinking skill:*** Integrating
    Sketch or name one place where all of these could be found.

**H**  **3 things often found in a suitcase**
- hair spray, hose, hems, handkerchief, Hushpuppy™ shoes

    ***Thinking skill:*** Problem solving
    Which would be the most appropriate item for Little Red Riding Hood to use to solve her wolf problem? Explain.

**I**  **2 things found in water**
- island, ice, instant tea

    ***Thinking skill:*** Estimation
    Estimate the amount in the world of each of your items.

**J**  **3 things you can buy**
- jam, jack-o-lantern, jump rope, Jeep™

    ***Thinking skill:*** Personal relevance
    Which item would you most want? Explain your rationale to the person next to you.

**K**  **2 things you can not buy**
- kingdom in England, kindness, knowledge

    ***Thinking skill:*** Ranking; elaboration
    Rank your list. Determine a situation in which that ranking would be significant.

**L**  **3 things in the newspaper**
- lines, lies, lovely pictures, little ads, lawyers

    ***Thinking skill:*** Frequency
    Which do you think is found the most frequently? Why?

**M**  **2 things found above ground**
- moon, machines, money

    ***Thinking skill:*** Observation
    Which could you best learn about through observation?

Kingore, B. (1999). <u>Integrating Thinking</u>. Austin, TX: Professional Associates.

**N** **2 things people do for a living**
- nursing, navigate, news reporting

*Thinking skill:* Inference
What is a valid inference that could be made about these things on your list?

**O** **2 things that are healthy**
- oxygen, oatmeal, old home remedies, organic foods

*Thinking skill:* Contrast
Circle two items on your list. Tell three ways they are different.

**P** **4 things people wear**
- pants, pink shirts, pins, parts (in hair)

*Thinking skill:* Serialization
Arrange your list in descending size.

**Q** **2 things smaller than a person**
- quail, quarter, quart of milk

*Thinking skill:* Magnify
Circle one item on your list. What would be the consequence if that item were actually larger than a person?

**R** **3 things that fly**
- robin, reindeer, rockets, red birds

*Thinking skill:* Minify
Circle one item on your list. Imagine that item as small as possible and discuss its use.

**S** **3 things that are hot**
- sun, stove, steam, summer school

*Thinking skill:* Substitute
Draw a sketch to show something that could be successfully substituted for one thing on your list.

**T** **2 things that make a noise**
- truck, turkeys, tractor, tiny tots

*Thinking skill:* Personal relevance
Explain which is the most important to you.

**U** **2 things to use outside**
- umbrella, unicycle, ultra-violet ray suntan lotion

*Thinking skill:* Evaluation
Judge which is most important for human comfort. Defend your choice to the person next to you.

**V** **3 things that are hard**
- vulture's beak, Volvo™, volcano, votive candle

*Thinking skill:* Cause and effect
Which would result in the most disastrous effect if it were soft instead of hard?

Kingore, B. (1999). Integrating Thinking. Austin, TX: Professional Associates.

**NOTES**

**W**  **2 things no one wants**
- warts, wasted time, wide waists

  *Thinking skill:* Elaboration
  Circle one item on your list. Write an eight to ten word sentence that explains why no one wants that thing.

**X**  **2 things that are not in this room**
- x-ray, xerox, xylophone

  *Thinking skill:* Integrating
  Name one place where all of these could be found.

**Y**  **2 things children can play with**
- yarn, yo-yo, yellow birds, youngsters

  *Thinking skill:* Attribute analysis
  List three attributes for one of your items.

**Z**  **2 things that can move**
- zebra, zoom lens, zipper

  *Thinking skill:* Personal analogy
  Circle one item on your list. Complete the analogy: "I am like _____ because..."

# FAST THOUGHTS: PETS

**P**  **2 kinds of pets**

**E**  **1 thing pets must do to survive**

**T**  **3 words to describe pets**

**S**  **2 places to find pets**

Kingore, B. (1999). <u>Integrating Thinking</u>. Austin, TX: Professional Associates.

# FAST THOUGHTS: RESEARCH

| R | 3 words to describe research |
|---|---|
| E | 2 sources of information |
| S | 2 kinds of information you can observe |
| E | 2 research topics appropriate to your grade level |
| A | 1 example of a kind of data you can infer |
| R | 2 important steps in research |
| C | 3 ways to share what you have learned in your research |
| H | 1 important term used in research |

Kingore, B. (1999). Integrating Thinking. Austin, TX: Professional Associates.

# FAST THOUGHTS: THINKING SKILLS

| A | **3 things that have teeth** |
|---|---|
| B | **2 things that break easily** |
| C | **4 things found at the zoo** |
| D | **2 things that have legs** |
| E | **2 things larger than a book** |
| F | **4 things you can eat** |
| G | **2 things you can not see** |
| H | **3 things often found in a suitcase** |
| I | **2 things found in water** |
| J | **3 things you can buy** |
| K | **2 things you can not buy** |
| L | **3 things in the newspaper** |

Kingore, B. (1999). Integrating Thinking. Austin, TX: Professional Associates.

| | |
|---|---|
| **M** | **2 things found above ground** |
| **N** | **2 things people do for a living** |
| **O** | **2 things that are healthy** |
| **P** | **4 things people wear** |
| **Q** | **2 things smaller than a person** |
| **R** | **3 things that fly** |
| **S** | **3 things that are hot** |
| **T** | **2 things that make a noise** |
| **U** | **2 things to use outside** |
| **V** | **3 things that are hard** |
| **W** | **2 things no one wants** |
| **X** | **2 things that are not in this room** |
| **Y** | **2 things children can play with** |
| **Z** | **2 things that can move** |

Kingore, B. (1999). Integrating Thinking. Austin, TX: Professional Associates.

# ACTION FIGURES

## PURPOSE

1. To actively engage students in whole body responses involving direction-ality, body parts, listening, and following directions

2. To assess students' ability to give directions in an appropriate, clear sequence for others to follow

**GRADE LEVELS:** K-8

## DESCRIPTION

Action figures are simple illustrations of figures in active poses. The figures are either used as overhead transparencies or enlarged and glued on card stock to make individual figure cards. Several classroom activities follow.

1. **Action Transitions.** Use individual figure cards as a transition with primary children. Hold up different cards and have the class move their bodies to match each pose. Later, show a numeral with the cards and create patterns for the children to follow, such as: "Do the first action pose two times and the second action pose three times."

2. **Following Direction Pairs.** Students stand face-to-face in pairs with one member of each pair facing the front of the room. Use the overhead or action figure cards to show one action figure. The students facing you use quiet voices to verbally explain to their partner who can not see the figure how to move their bodies to match the pose. Next, have the partners switch places and show a different action figure for those students to explain. Much discussion and laughter often accompany this task!

3. **Writing Directions.** Each student has a copy of one action figure. Students write directions that enable someone to get into that pose without seeing the drawing. After completing the writing tasks, students read each others directions, move their bodies to follow the directions, and try to match the action figure pose without seeing it. Next, students view the drawing and discuss any discrepancies between the drawing and the directions. Students then offer suggestions to each other to increase the clarity of the written directions. Finally, encourage students to revise their directions and retest their writing by asking another student or another class to read and follow their directions.

Kingore, B. (1999). Integrating Thinking. Austin, TX: Professional Associates.

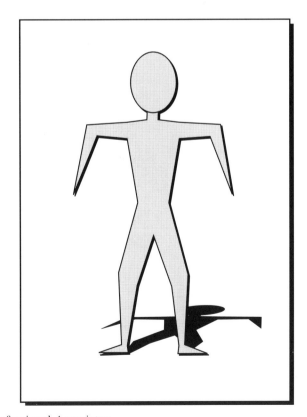

Kingore, B. (1999). <u>Integrating Thinking</u>. Austin, TX: Professional Associates.

Kingore, B. (1999). <u>Integrating Thinking</u>. Austin, TX: Professional Associates.

Kingore, B. (1999). <u>Integrating Thinking</u>. Austin, TX: Professional Associates.

# VENN VARIATIONS

## PURPOSE

1. To enable students to compare and contrast by analyzing similarities and differences

2. To enable teachers to encourage and assess students' depth and complexity of information

**GRADE LEVELS:** K-1 with teacher facilitating; 2-12 independently

## DESCRIPTION

A Venn Diagram compares how things are different and how they are similar. On the classic Venn with two overlapping ovals such as the one below, information is organized by listing in the ovals the attributes of each item; the attributes common to both items are listed in the overlapping area.

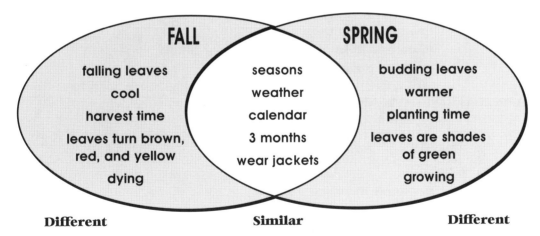

**Different**                    **Similar**                    **Different**

Vary the form of the Venn so it can be used frequently without becoming mundane. Several variations, some completed examples, and blank forms of these variations are included to model possibilities.

## VENN VARIATIONS

1. **Vertical Venn.**
   Use the Venn vertically instead of horizontally. This change provides a wider area for students to write in more legibly.

Kingore, B. (1999). <u>Integrating Thinking</u>. Austin, TX: Professional Associates.

2. **Three-dimensional Venn.**
   - **Overlapping circles.** Use wide yarn to form large, overlapping circles on carpet or felt boards. The yarn adheres to carpet and felt surfaces and allows the comparison of large manipulatives.
   - **Hula Hoops.** Two hula hoops can overlap on the floor to form large manipulative areas for comparing concrete items.

3. **Three-way Venn.**
   Overlap three circles to create a Three-way Venn. Have students outline each circle in a different color to make overlapping areas more distinctive. Then, use the Three-way Venn to expand comparisons and enhance the complexity and depth of information about a topic or three different items.

4. **Topic-shaped Venn.**
   Use overlapping outlines of two different objects to form a Venn. Overlapping shapes provide a topic-related challenge that assesses under-standing of each item and the relationships between items. Variations such as the following have proven effective.

   - **Insect--**Three body parts are used as Venn areas
   - **A bow tie**
   - **Vehicles--**Overlap an airplane and a boat or other transportation vehicles to compare their attributes
   - **Geometric shapes**
   - **Fruit and vegetable**
   - **Plant and animal**
   - **Two countries, states, or regions**

**APPLICATIONS OF VENN VARIATIONS**

Use Venn variations to compare a myriad of things including the following suggestions.

   - **Books by the same author**
   - **Different resources about the same topic**
   - **Expository and narrative writing**
   - **Math operations**
   - **Versions of the same story**
   - **Characters or historical figures**
   - **Past and present**
   - **Geographic regions**
   - **Opposites**
   - **Events**
   - **Tools**
   - **Simple and complex machines**
   - **Food groups**

Kingore, B. (1999). <u>Integrating Thinking</u>. Austin, TX: Professional Associates.

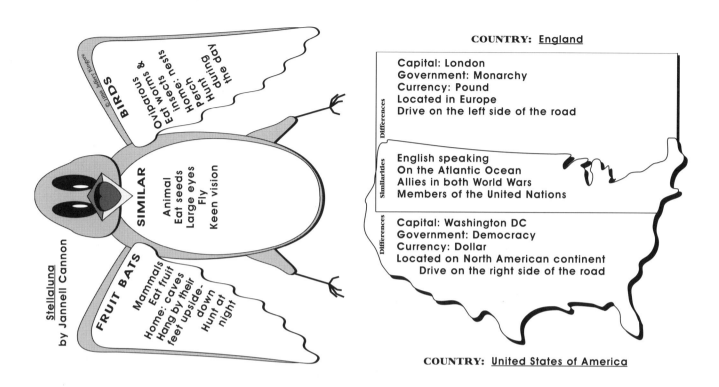

**BIRDS**

Oviparous &
Eat worms &
insects
Home: nests
Perch
Hunting during
the day

© 1986 Lenny Long

**SIMILAR**

Animal
Eat seeds
Large eyes
Fly
Keen vision

*Stellaluna*
by Jannell Cannon

**FRUIT BATS**

Mammals
Eat fruit
Home: caves
Hang by their
feet upside-
down
Hunt at
night

**COUNTRY:** <u>England</u>

**Differences**

Capital: London
Government: Monarchy
Currency: Pound
Located in Europe
Drive on the left side of the road

**Similarities**

English speaking
On the Atlantic Ocean
Allies in both World Wars
Members of the United Nations

**Differences**

Capital: Washington DC
Government: Democracy
Currency: Dollar
Located on North American continent
Drive on the right side of the road

**COUNTRY:** <u>United States of America</u>

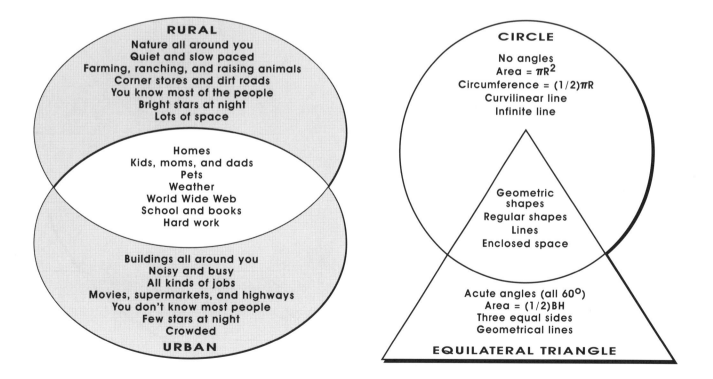

**RURAL**
Nature all around you
Quiet and slow paced
Farming, ranching, and raising animals
Corner stores and dirt roads
You know most of the people
Bright stars at night
Lots of space

Homes
Kids, moms, and dads
Pets
Weather
World Wide Web
School and books
Hard work

Buildings all around you
Noisy and busy
All kinds of jobs
Movies, supermarkets, and highways
You don't know most people
Few stars at night
Crowded
**URBAN**

**CIRCLE**

No angles
Area = $\pi R^2$
Circumference = $(1/2)\pi R$
Curvilinear line
Infinite line

Geometric
shapes
Regular shapes
Lines
Enclosed space

Acute angles (all 60°)
Area = $(1/2)BH$
Three equal sides
Geometrical lines

**EQUILATERAL TRIANGLE**

Kingore, B. (1999). <u>Integrating Thinking</u>. Austin, TX: Professional Associates.

# VERTICAL VENN:
# COMPARE AND CONTRAST

NAME _____   DATE _____

TOPIC _____

**DIFFERENT**

**SIMILAR**

**DIFFERENT**

Kingore, B. (1999). Integrating Thinking. Austin, TX: Professional Associates.

## BOOK COVER:
## COMPARE AND CONTRAST

NAME _____ DATE _____

TOPIC _____

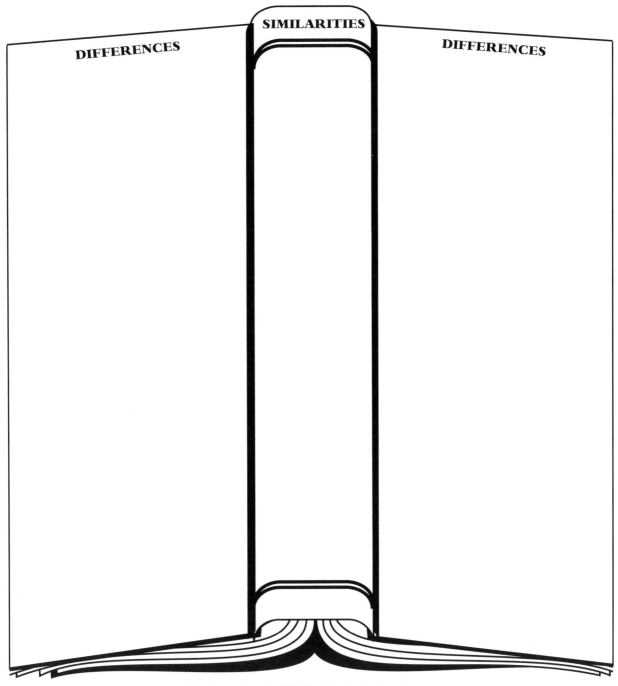

**SIMILARITIES**

**DIFFERENCES**

**DIFFERENCES**

Kingore, B. (1999). Integrating Thinking. Austin, TX: Professional Associates.

# THREE-WAY VENN:
# COMPARE AND CONTRAST

NAME _____     DATE _____

TOPIC_____

Kingore, B. (1999). <u>Integrating Thinking</u>. Austin, TX: Professional Associates.

# BIRD:
# COMPARE AND CONTRAST

NAME _____ DATE _____

TOPIC _____

DIFFERENT

© 1999 Jeffery Kingore

SIMILAR

DIFFERENT

Kingore, B. (1999). <u>Integrating Thinking</u>. Austin, TX: Professional Associates.

# COUNTRIES, STATES OR REGIONS: COMPARE AND CONTRAST ▬▬▬

NAME _____     DATE _____

TOPIC _____

**COUNTRY:** _____

**DIFFERENCES**

**SIMILARITIES**

**DIFFERENCES**

**COUNTRY:** _United States of America_

Kingore, B. (1999). <u>Integrating Thinking</u>. Austin, TX: Professional Associates.

# REFERENCES

Cannon, J. (1993). <u>Stellaluna</u>. New York: Harcourt Brace.

Hoffman, M. (1991). <u>Amazing Grace</u>. New York: Dial.

Kingore, B. (1999). <u>Assessment: Time Saving Procedures for Busy Teachers</u>. 2nd ed. Austin, TX: Professional Associates.

Kingore, B. (1995). <u>Reaching High Potentials</u>. Worthington, OH: Macmillian/McGraw-Hill.

Macon, JM.; Bewell, D.; and Voyt, ME. (1991). <u>Responses to Literature</u>. Newark, DE: International Reading Association.

Marshall, J. (1985). <u>Miss Nelson Has a Field Day</u>. Boston: Houghton-Mifflin.

Marshall, J. (1977). <u>Miss Nelson Is Missing</u>. Boston: Houghton-Mifflin.

Scieszka, J. (1989). <u>The True Story of the 3 Little Pigs!</u> New York: Viking.

Spinelli, J. (1990). <u>Maniac Cagee</u>. New York: Scholastic.